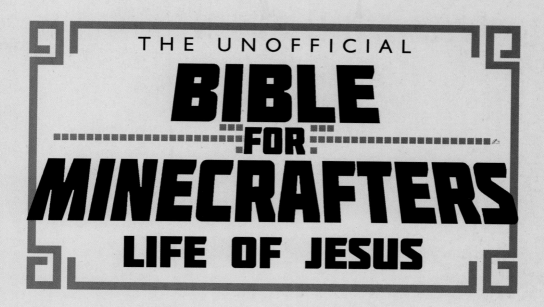

THE UNOFFICIAL
BIBLE
FOR
MINECRAFTERS
LIFE OF JESUS

GARRETT ROMINES AND CHRISTOPHER MIKO

STORIES FROM THE BIBLE
TOLD BLOCK BY BLOCK

LION

Published by
Lion Hudson Limited
Wilkinson House, Jordan Hill Business Park
Banbury Road, Oxford OX2 8DR, England
www.lionhudson.com

ISBN 978 0 7459 7731 7

Original Bible edition published by Sky Pony Press, 307 West 36th Street, 11th Floor, New York, NY 10018

Stories originally published in *The Unofficial Old Testament for Minecrafters* and *The Unofficial New Testament for Minecrafters* 2016
This mini edition 2017

Acknowledgments
A catalogue record for this book is available from the British Library
Minecraft ® is a registered trademark of Notch Development AB.
The Minecraft ® game is copyright © Mojang AB.

Printed and bound in China, December 2018, LH54

CONTENTS

FOREWORD

I'm always on the lookout for new ways to tell Bible stories. That's what storytellers do. The hardest job is finding a compelling and original "way in" to a story. And when I find something that works, I get really excited.

A few years back, the publishers behind the original US edition of these books created *The Brick Bible*. My son immediately went out and bought a copy. So OK, he's 33, but he's a LEGO ® fanatic, and he thought that the idea was absolutely brilliant!

He may not be quite so keen on Minecraft ®, but my grandchildren are. They don't get much game-playing time, but when they do, Minecraft ® is their first choice. The older two (nine and six) love building the worlds, while the youngest, who is only three, simply enjoys digging holes and getting stuck in them.

So when I showed them a few sample pages from *The Unofficial Bible for Minecrafters*, they got the same look on their faces that my son had on his when he found *The Brick Bible*. Their responses ranged from "It's funny" (which it is!) to "When can I read some more?"

As for me, I turned the pages just to see what the creators of the book would get up to next and how they would bring each scene to Minecrafter-life. And I have to say that I was surprised and delighted.

Every now and then, someone comes up with a new way of telling Bible stories that is just that little bit different. And if this is a "way in" for someone (and there are thousands of Minecrafters out there) and it's compelling, intriguing, and faithful to the text, then I'm happy to recommend it. That's what storytellers do.

Bob Hartman

Bob Hartman, Storyteller

THE BIRTH OF JESUS

Matthew 1–2; Luke 1–2

Hi God!

Hello Gabriel.

Here comes your Son!

MARY WAS A YOUNG GIRL, ENGAGED TO BE MARRIED TO JOSEPH. ONE DAY THE ANGEL GABRIEL APPEARED, TELLING HER SHE WOULD HAVE A BABY. AND SOON AFTERWARDS MARY FOUND SHE WAS PREGNANT.

JOSEPH DID NOT WANT TO EXPOSE MARY TO PUBLIC DISGRACE AND DECIDED TO BREAK OFF THEIR ENGAGEMENT QUIETLY. BUT AN ANGEL APPEARED TO JOSEPH IN A DREAM AND TOLD HIM TO MARRY MARY.

THE EMPEROR AUGUSTUS ISSUED A DECREE THAT EVERYONE HAD TO REGISTER IN THEIR HOME TOWN. SO JOSEPH JOURNEYED TO BETHLEHEM WITH MARY.

JOSEPH AND MARY TRIED TO FIND LODGINGS BUT THE ROOMS AT THE INN WERE ALREADY TAKEN. SO THEY ENDED UP SPENDING THE NIGHT IN A STABLE.

Sir, I know you have said that you are full, but my wife is expecting a child and I'm sure it will come soon.

The best I can do is my stable.

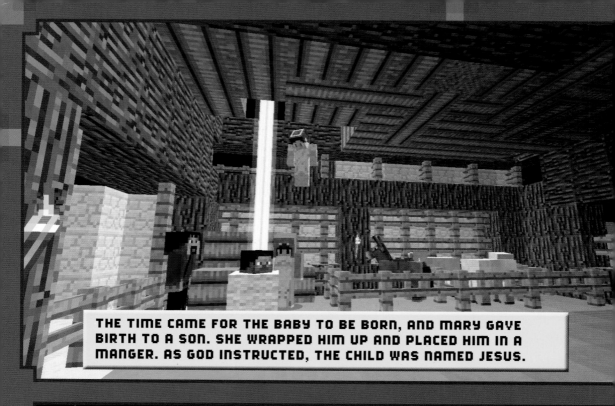

THE TIME CAME FOR THE BABY TO BE BORN, AND MARY GAVE BIRTH TO A SON. SHE WRAPPED HIM UP AND PLACED HIM IN A MANGER. AS GOD INSTRUCTED, THE CHILD WAS NAMED JESUS.

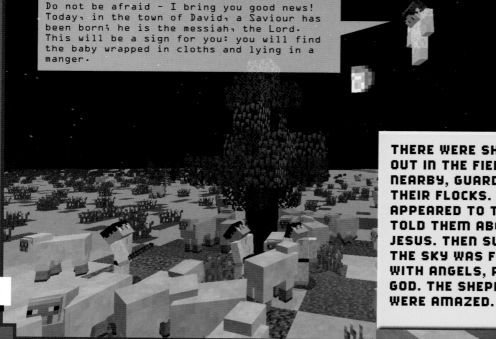

Do not be afraid - I bring you good news! Today, in the town of David, a Saviour has been born; he is the messiah, the Lord. This will be a sign for you: you will find the baby wrapped in cloths and lying in a manger.

THERE WERE SHEPHERDS OUT IN THE FIELDS NEARBY, GUARDING THEIR FLOCKS. AN ANGEL APPEARED TO THEM AND TOLD THEM ABOUT BABY JESUS. THEN SUDDENLY THE SKY WAS FILLED WITH ANGELS, PRAISING GOD. THE SHEPHERDS WERE AMAZED.

Let's go and see the messiah for ourselves.

It's a miracle!

THE ANGELS LEFT AND THE SHEPHERDS HURRIED TO BETHLEHEM. THERE THEY FOUND BABY JESUS LYING IN THE MANGER.

The baby we saw is the messiah!

THE SHEPHERDS TOLD EVERYONE THEY SAW ABOUT THE CHILD AND ALL WERE AMAZED.

AFTER THE BIRTH OF JESUS, A STAR APPEARED. WISE MEN FROM THE EAST BELIEVED A KING HAD BEEN BORN AND SET OUT TO FOLLOW THE STAR. IN JERUSALEM, THEY ASKED WHERE THEY COULD FIND THE CHILD AND WERE TOLD TO GO TO BETHLEHEM. SO THEY JOURNEYED ON WITH THE STAR AHEAD OF THEM, UNTIL IT STOPPED ABOVE THE PLACE WHERE JESUS WAS.

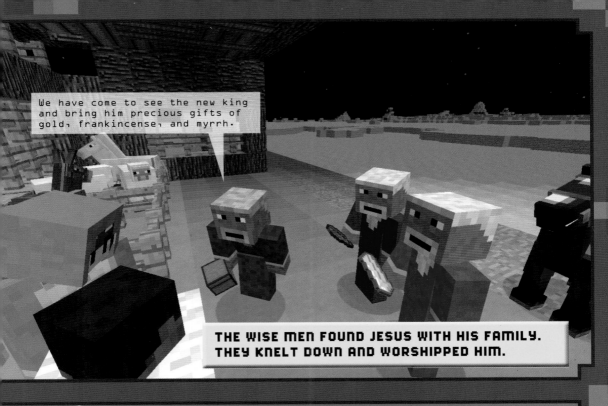

We have come to see the new king and bring him precious gifts of gold, frankincense, and myrrh.

THE WISE MEN FOUND JESUS WITH HIS FAMILY. THEY KNELT DOWN AND WORSHIPPED HIM.

THE WISE MEN BEGAN THEIR JOURNEY HOME, OVERCOME WITH JOY AT WHAT THEY HAD SEEN.

THE BOY JESUS
AT THE TEMPLE
Luke 2

Even as a boy, he is starting to do amazing things.

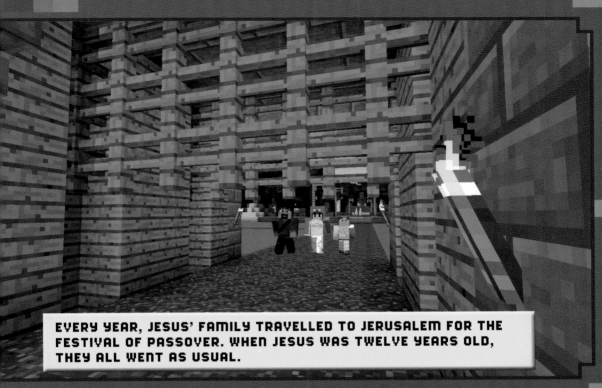

EVERY YEAR, JESUS' FAMILY TRAVELLED TO JERUSALEM FOR THE FESTIVAL OF PASSOVER. WHEN JESUS WAS TWELVE YEARS OLD, THEY ALL WENT AS USUAL.

AFTER THE FESTIVAL, WHILE JESUS' PARENTS WERE GETTING READY TO GO HOME, THE YOUNG BOY WENT OUT TO THE TEMPLE ON HIS OWN.

JOSEPH AND MARY WERE SO BUSY PREPARING TO LEAVE, AND THERE WERE SO MANY PEOPLE TRAVELLING IN THE SAME GROUP, THEY DID NOT NOTICE THAT JESUS WASN'T WITH THEM.

I haven't seen Jesus in a while!

Mary, the boy is far more capable than you or I. He is probably at the back with the other kids.

AFTER WALKING FOR SEVERAL HOURS, MARY AND JOSEPH REALIZED THAT THEY HAD NO IDEA WHERE JESUS WAS.

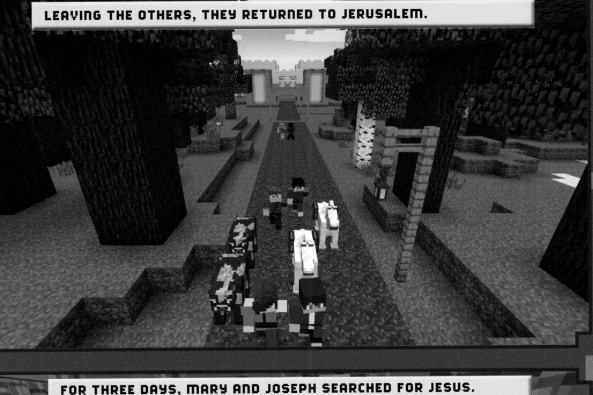

FOR THREE DAYS, MARY AND JOSEPH SEARCHED FOR JESUS. FINALLY, THEY FOUND OUT HE WAS AT THE TEMPLE COURTS.

We are looking for our son. He is twelve.

Excuse me, have you seen our son?

11

JOSEPH AND MARY HURRIED TO THE TEMPLE COURTS.

What's going on?

Look at that boy over there, talking to the teachers. They can't believe how intelligent and wise he is.

WHEN JESUS' PARENTS SAW HIM, THEY WERE ASTONISHED AND VERY PROUD. JESUS, THE SON OF GOD, WAS TEACHING IN HIS FATHER'S HOME.

JESUS HEALS THE SICK
Luke 5

Wow - it didn't take long for Jesus to become popular.

WHEN JESUS GREW UP, HE BEGAN TO PREACH. WHEREVER JESUS WENT, PEOPLE GATHERED TO HEAR HIM SPEAK.

For everyone who asks, receives. Everyone who seeks, finds. And to everyone who knocks, the door will be opened.

A GROUP CARRIED A PARALYSED MAN ON A BED TO LAY HIM BEFORE JESUS.

WHEN THEY COULD NOT FIND A WAY THROUGH THE CROWD, THEY WENT UP ON THE ROOF AND LOWERED HIM ON HIS BED.

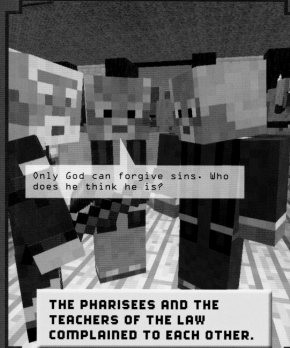

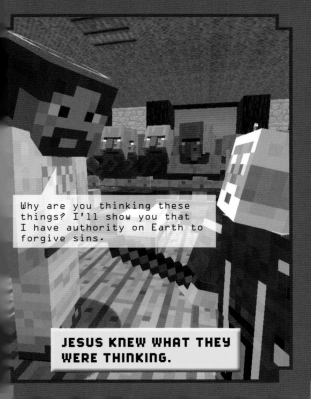

15

I can stand. I can walk!

IMMEDIATELY, THE MAN WAS HEALED.

JESUS FEEDS 5,000 PEOPLE
Matthew 14

That's amazing!

Wait until you see
what he does next!

Master, the people must be hungry. We should let them go away to the nearest towns and find food.

ONE EVENING, THE DISCIPLES CAME TO SPEAK TO JESUS. ALL DAY JESUS HAD HEALED PEOPLE AND NOW IT WAS LATE.

There is no need for them to go; give them what we have.

JESUS ASKED THE DISCIPLES TO BRING HIM THE SMALL AMOUNT OF FOOD THAT THEY HAD.

All we have here is five loaves and two fish.

JESUS SAID A PRAYER OF THANKS AND THEN GAVE THE LOAVES AND FISH TO THE DISCIPLES TO DISTRIBUTE AMONG THE PEOPLE.

It's a miracle!

THE DISCIPLES PASSED AROUND THE BREAD AND FISH, BUT IT DID NOT RUN OUT.

THERE WERE OVER 5,000 PEOPLE IN THE CROWD, AND THEY ALL ATE TO THEIR HEART'S CONTENT. THE SCRAPS LEFT OVER WERE ENOUGH TO FILL TWELVE GREAT BASKETS.

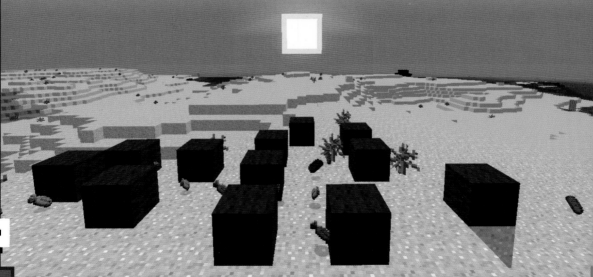

JESUS WALKS ON WATER
Matthew 14

Is there anything Jesus can't do? He's so talented!

Like Father, like Son!

THE SUN WAS SETTING AND JESUS TOLD THE DISCIPLES TO GO ON AHEAD OF HIM BY BOAT TO THE OTHER SIDE OF THE LAKE. JESUS THEN WENT UP THE HILLSIDE TO PRAY ALONE.

SEVERAL HOURS LATER, THE DISCIPLES SAW SOMETHING IN THE DISTANCE.

Come and join me!

AS THE SUN BEGAN TO RISE, THEY SAW JESUS COMING TOWARD THEM. HE WAS WALKING ON THE WATER!

JESUS GOES TO JERUSALEM
Matthew 21

On to Jerusalem!

Yes, that's right! Enough groundwork has been laid. Jesus is ready to begin the end.

The end?

Go into the village that is just ahead, and you will find a donkey tied to a post. Untie it and bring it to me.

THE TIME OF PASSOVER WAS APPROACHING, AND JESUS AND HIS DISCIPLES WERE ON THEIR WAY TO JERUSALEM. JESUS TOLD TWO OF HIS DISCIPLES TO GO ON AHEAD TO THE NEAREST VILLAGE.

THIS WAS FORETOLD THROUGH THE PROPHET, WHO SAID: "LOOK – YOUR KING IS COMING TO YOU... RIDING ON A DONKEY."

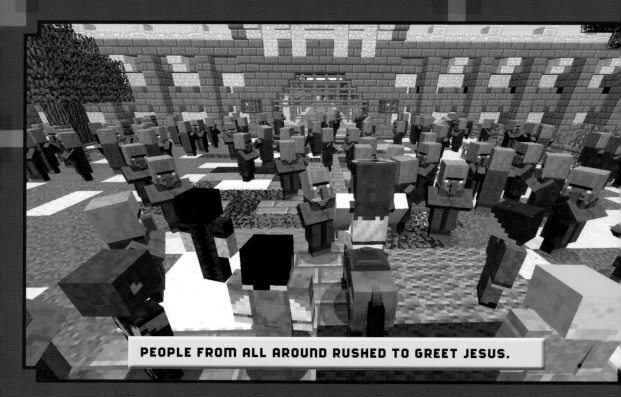

PEOPLE FROM ALL AROUND RUSHED TO GREET JESUS.

HE TRIUMPHANTLY ENTERED JERUSALEM. PEOPLE LAID THEIR CLOAKS AND PALM LEAVES ON THE GROUND BEFORE HIM.

ONCE JESUS ENTERED THE CITY, HE MADE HIS WAY TO THE TEMPLE. HE WAS FILLED WITH OUTRAGE AT WHAT HE SAW: THERE WERE MONEY CHANGERS AND PEOPLE BUYING AND SELLING WARES IN ORDER TO MAKE A PROFIT. JESUS GRABBED A ROPE.

Get out of my Father's house!

HE DROVE OUT ALL WHO WERE BUYING AND SELLING THERE.

LATER, THE BLIND AND THE LAME CAME TO JESUS AT THE TEMPLE, AND HE HEALED THEM. THE CHIEF PRIESTS AND TEACHERS OF THE LAW WERE INDIGNANT WHEN THEY HEARD CHILDREN PRAISING JESUS.

JESUS' FINAL DAYS

Matthew 26–27; Luke 23

The crucial moment has arrived. My plan will be fulfilled.

It's not going to be easy, is it?

No - his greatest challenges are ahead of him.

ON THE FIRST DAY OF THE FESTIVAL, THE DISCIPLES MADE ARRANGEMENTS, FOLLOWING JESUS' INSTRUCTIONS, TO CELEBRATE THE PASSOVER MEAL AT THE HOUSE OF A MAN IN THE CITY.

WHILE THEY WERE EATING, JESUS REVEALED THAT ONE OF THEM WOULD BETRAY HIM. JUDAS PRETENDED NOT TO KNOW ANYTHING ABOUT IT.

Take this bread and eat it; this is my body. Take this cup and drink from it, all of you. This is my blood of the covenant, which is poured out for many, for the forgiveness of sins.

JESUS TOOK SOME BREAD AND SAID A PRAYER OF THANKS. THEN HE BROKE IT AND DIVIDED IT AMONG THE DISCIPLES. NEXT HE TOOK A CUP OF WINE AND BLESSED IT. JESUS HANDED IT TO THE DISCIPLES AND THEY ALL DRANK FROM IT.

Who is it you want?

Jesus of Nazareth.

LATER THAT EVENING, JESUS LEFT WITH HIS DISCIPLES AND WENT TO THE GARDEN OF GETHSEMANE TO PRAY AND REFLECT. MUCH LATER JUDAS CAME TO THE GARDEN, TOGETHER WITH SOLDIERS FROM THE CHIEF PRIESTS AND THE PHARISEES. THEY CARRIED TORCHES, LANTERNS, AND WEAPONS. THE SOLDIERS ARRESTED JESUS.

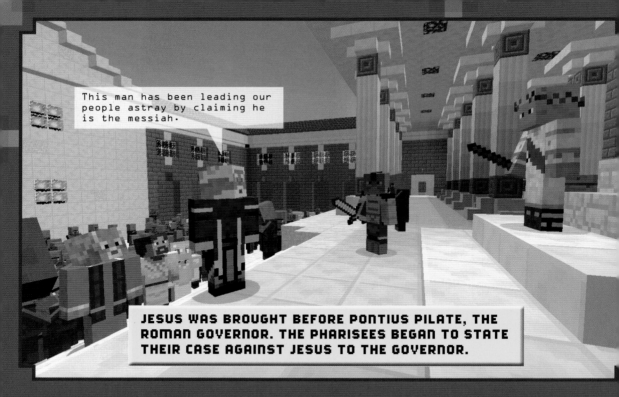

This man has been leading our people astray by claiming he is the messiah.

JESUS WAS BROUGHT BEFORE PONTIUS PILATE, THE ROMAN GOVERNOR. THE PHARISEES BEGAN TO STATE THEIR CASE AGAINST JESUS TO THE GOVERNOR.

Are you the king of the Jews?

Does this question come from you or have other people told you about me?

PILATE TOOK JESUS INTO HIS PALACE TO QUESTION HIM BUT HE COULD NOT FIND A REASON TO KILL HIM. BUT THE CROWD OUTSIDE CRIED "KILL HIM! KILL HIM!" SO HE SENTENCED JESUS TO CRUCIFIXION.

JESUS WAS HANDED OVER TO THE ROMAN SOLDIERS. HE WAS THEN STRIPPED AND BEATEN, AND A CROWN OF THORNS WAS PLACED ON HIS HEAD.

NEXT, JESUS CARRIED HIS CROSS THROUGH THE CITY, HEADING OUT TO GOLGOTHA, WHICH MEANS "THE PLACE OF THE SKULL".

OTHER CRIMINALS WERE LED OUT TO BE EXECUTED ALONG WITH JESUS. WHEN THEY CAME TO GOLGOTHA, THE SOLDIERS NAILED JESUS TO THE CROSS AND SET IT UPRIGHT. THE CRIMINALS WERE ALSO HUNG ON CROSSES — ONE TO THE RIGHT OF JESUS AND ONE TO THE LEFT.

ONE OF THE CRIMINALS HANGING BESIDE JESUS STARTED TO
MOCK AND INSULT HIM, BUT THE OTHER MAN SPOKE HUMBLY.

THE DEATH AND RESURRECTION OF JESUS

Matthew 27–28; Luke 23–24

I can't look... I have to turn away.

I know. But this was all part of the plan...

By this time it was afternoon, and darkness fell across the whole land. The light from the sun was gone. Then Jesus cried out, and with those words he breathed his last living breath.

JESUS WAS LAID IN A TOMB AND A HEAVY STONE WAS ROLLED IN FRONT OF THE ENTRANCE.

He's gone! All that's left is his white cloth!

How did that happen?

VERY EARLY ON SUNDAY MORNING, MARY, JESUS' MOTHER, AND MARY MAGDALENE TOOK THE SPICES THEY HAD PREPARED AND WENT TO THE TOMB. THEY WERE VERY SURPRISED TO FIND THAT THE STONE HAD BEEN ROLLED AWAY FROM THE TOMB, AND, WHEN THEY ENTERED, THEY COULD NOT SEE JESUS' BODY. SUDDENLY, TWO MEN IN DAZZLINGLY WHITE CLOTHES STOOD IN FRONT OF THEM. "HE IS NOT HERE," THEY SAID. "HE HAS RISEN AS WAS WRITTEN IN THE SCRIPTURES!"

It's true - Jesus has risen from the dead!

Yeah, right!

THE WOMEN RUSHED TO TELL THE DISCIPLES ALL THAT THEY HAD SEEN.

PETER RAN TO THE TOMB AND SAW THAT IT WAS EMPTY, EXCEPT FOR THE WHITE LINEN CLOTH.

JESUS IS TAKEN UP TO HEAVEN

Matthew 28; Luke 24; John 20; Acts 1

You see, I told you it would all work out.

WHILE JESUS WAS AT THE TABLE WITH THEM, HE TOOK BREAD, GAVE THANKS, BROKE IT, AND BEGAN TO SHARE IT WITH THEM. THEIR EYES OPENED WIDE AS THEY FINALLY RECOGNIZED HIM, BUT HE QUICKLY DISAPPEARED FROM THEIR SIGHT.

AT ONCE, THEY RETURNED TO JERUSALEM. THERE THEY FOUND THE OTHER DISCIPLES AND TOLD THEM WHAT HAD HAPPENED. THEN JESUS HIMSELF APPEARED AMONG THEM TO GIVE THEM AN IMPORTANT MESSAGE.

JESUS THEN LEFT THEM AND WAS TAKEN UP TO HEAVEN.